Copyright © 2022 by Floydise Paquette

Published by Grace Koinonia Publishing
10926 Quality Drive
Suite 38175
Charlotte, NC 28278

All rights reserved under International Copyright Law. Contents and/or cover may not be reproduced or shared in whole or in part in any form, stored in a retrieval system, or transmitted in any form by any means—electronic, mechanical, photocopy, recording, scanning or otherwise—without the expressed written consent of the author.

It is expressly prohibited to forward the electronic copy of this work via email or any other means to another user.

This work is sold with the understanding that neither the publisher nor the author are engaged in rendering professional advice or services. If professional assistance is required, the services of a professional person should be sought.

The fact that an individual is referred to in this work as a citation does not mean that the author endorses or agrees with any other information or views the individual may hold outside of the specific quotation used.

All rights reserved.
ISBN-978-1-7364781-0-3

THIS BOOK BELONGS TO:

_____

GOALS JOURNAL & WORKBOOK

SECTIONS:

THE WORKING PIECES OF YOUR GOALS JOURNAL & WORKBOOK

1. MY VISION
2. MY GOAL
3. WHAT DO I NEED TO GET STARTED?
4. WHAT'S MY PLAN?
5. WHERE AM I NOW?
6. CHECK IN: HOW AM I FEELING?
7. WHAT WILL THIS CHANGE DO FOR ME?
8. WHAT ARE THE CHALLENGES I MIGHT FACE?

GOALS JOURNAL & WORKBOOK

SECTIONS:
THE WORKING PIECES OF YOUR GOALS JOURNAL & WORKBOOK

- 9 — HOW WILL I OVERCOME THESE CHALLENGES?
- 10 — DO I NEED HELP? DO I NEED ACCOUNTABILITY?
- 11 — LETTER OF ENCOURAGEMENT
- 12 — MY TASK TRACKER
- 13 — MY INSPIRATION
- 14 — MY RESULTS!
- 15 — CHECK IN: HOW AM I FEELING?
- 16 — LESSONS I LEARNED

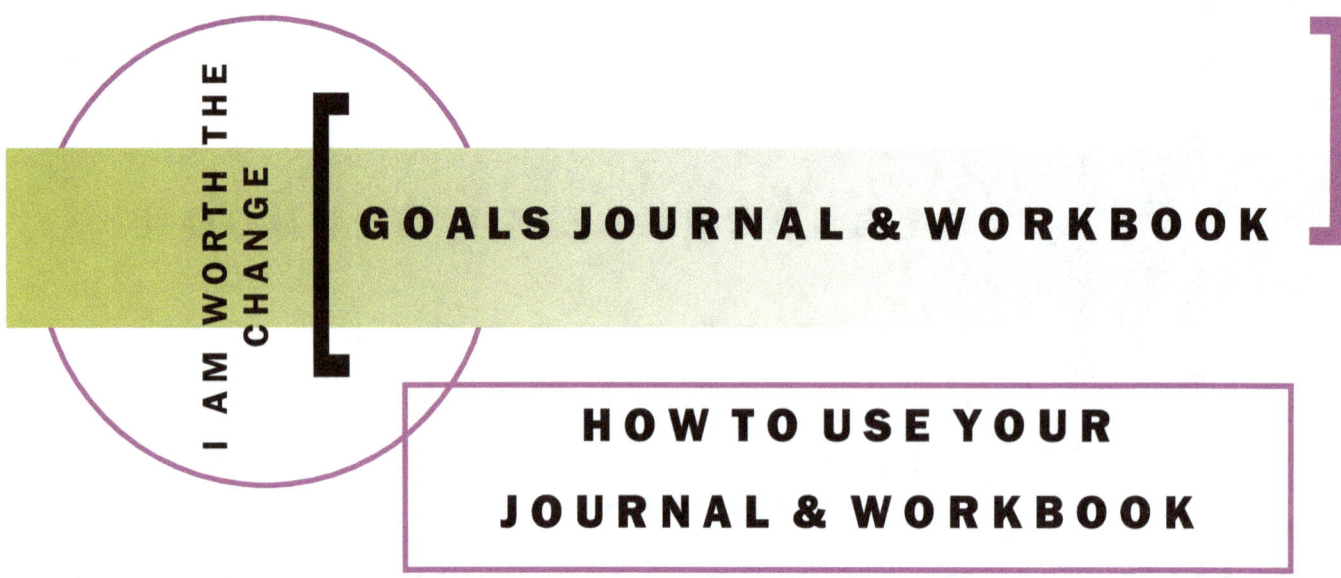

HOW TO USE YOUR JOURNAL & WORKBOOK

Note: This is just encouraging guidance to get the most out of your goals journal and workbook. I really want you to make it your own. There is so much you will discover on this journey.

1 — MY VISION

This is the most important part of the goals process. It is the foundation on which your goals are set. Your vision keeps you balanced and on course. When challenges arise, your vision sees you through.

You don't have to write a separate vision for each goal; each goal lines up with the vision you have for your life. This doesn't mean each goal looks similar, it just means each goal has a purpose and is divinely connected to your destiny.

Your vision is special insight into your destiny.

Take your time with it. Impatience and rushing to "just get it done" can take the joy out of it. Don't rob yourself of the beautiful moments you have to be still, wait for clarity and then record your vision.

This is where you get to live out loud and unlimited. Remove the limitations and the impossibilities. Remove the boxes and push pause on your fears and insecurities.

For the creatives, feel free to create a vision board to get your juices flowing.

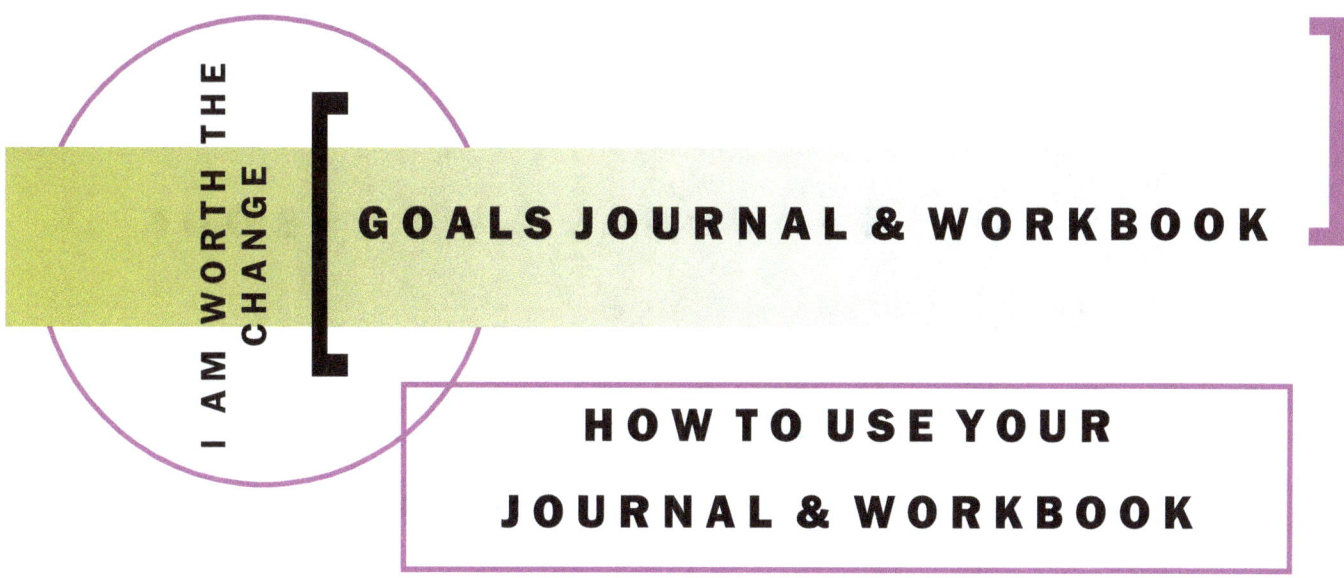

HOW TO USE YOUR JOURNAL & WORKBOOK

Other ways to get your vision out of your heart might be to write a poem, journal, write a song, or pray and ask God to help you and show you what He created you for.

2 — MY GOAL

You can have goals for your family, your marriage, your children, a business, a ministry, a non-profit organization, education, self-development, a community initiative, etc.

Let me say this: You do not have to work on multiple goals all at once and you don't have to only work on one goal at a time.

Consider your life's vision. Your life's vision helps to guide you when creating your goals, so you don't get distracted. Your vision keeps you from experiencing FOMO (Fear of Missing Out), falling into shiny object syndrome and running off chasing something else on a whim. Your life's vision is a continual source of encouragement that lets you know you are on the right track.

When setting your goals, ask yourself: Does it align with my vision? Keep in mind, this question shouldn't create limitations. Ask yourself: Do I really want this and why? Oftentimes, your answer will help open up your vision and bring more clarity.

Your why is very important. Be honest with yourself. You might discover your why is tied to people pleasing. You might discover you are tied to your why because it makes you "feel" successful, which ultimately has the potential to draw you away from your real life goals. On the other hand, you might discover your why is tied to the hope that lies deep in your heart and you didn't even

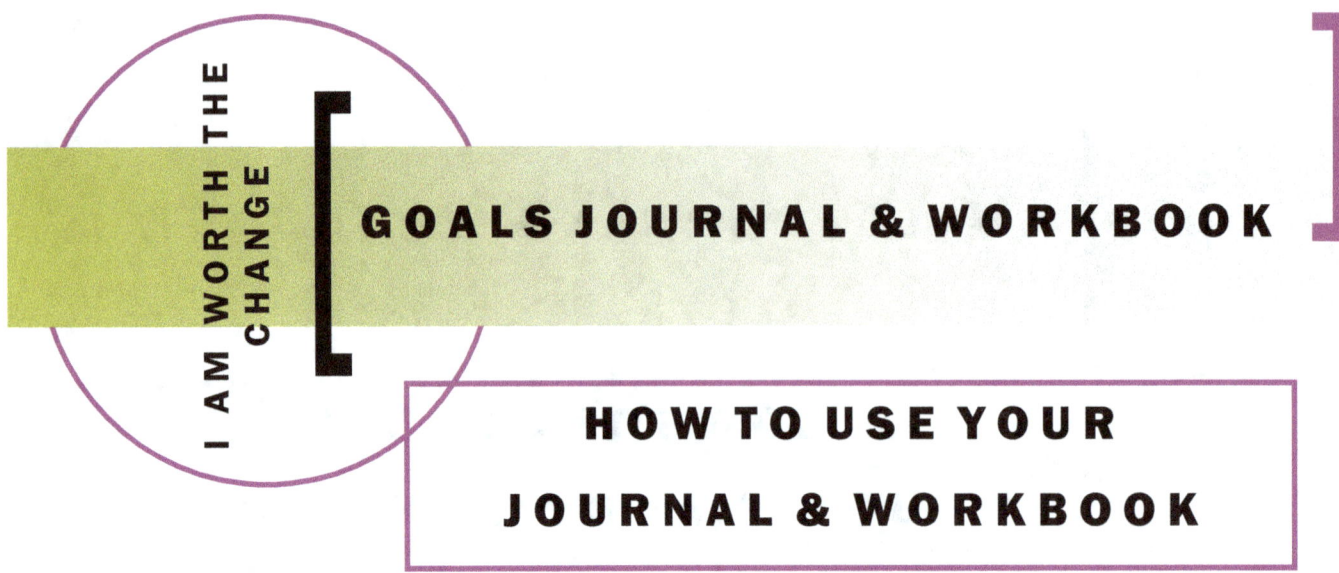

GOALS JOURNAL & WORKBOOK

HOW TO USE YOUR JOURNAL & WORKBOOK

know it had so much meaning to you. Ask why for each goal, go deep with it—you may be surprised at the treasures you uncover and the healing that takes place in your heart. It will also help shape your response to section 7, "What Will This Change Do For Me?"

 WHAT DO I NEED TO GET STARTED?

What Do I Need to Get Started?

You may have both internal & external needs.

Sometimes what you need to get started won't be found outside of your reach. What you may need is the right mindset—the right attitude. No matter what goal you set, big or small, if you start with a defeated mindset, it will be difficult to obtain victory. Your mind can't be the thing working against you. So before you go outside of you, buying a bunch of stuff, take the time to invest in you. A sound mind is priceless and it's something you can't buy.

Your external needs are practical things. In light of your goal, ask yourself these questions:

1. What is it going to take?
2. Can I make it work with what I already have? Be creative.
3. Do I need to purchase anything? If so, is it an absolute requirement at this time or can it wait? Can I improvise?
4. What do I need to learn?

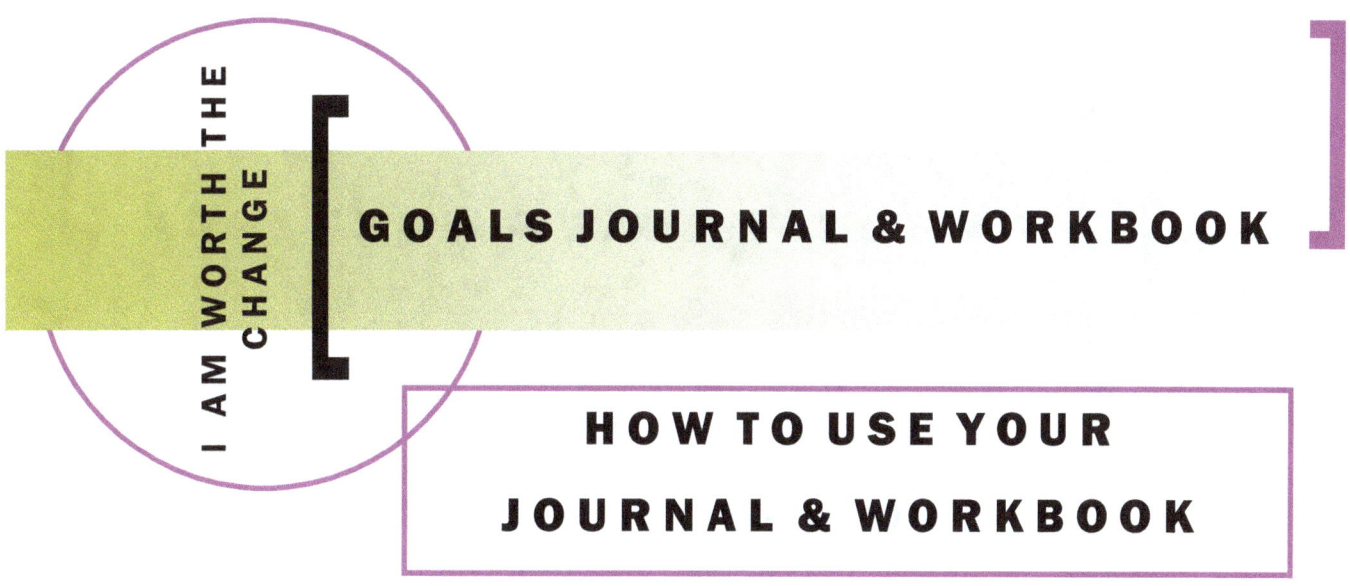

HOW TO USE YOUR JOURNAL & WORKBOOK

4 — WHAT'S MY PLAN?

Step by Step: Starting Point ⇨ Sustainability ⇨ Growth

Consider the needs you identified in part 3, "What Do I Need to Get Started?" Then, ask yourself, what one small step can I take to get the ball rolling? What would the next necessary step be? And the next? These will likely get plugged into your Task Tracker.

Next, ask yourself what sustainability looks like for this goal. Then, ask yourself what step you can take towards it.

Lastly, ask yourself what growth looks like for the goal. Then, ask yourself what step you can take towards it.

Your plan is not another space for what you need, but to write down <u>how</u> you're going to accomplish your goal.

Remember, this is not a rush or a race. It's a process. Give yourself grace and go with the flow.

5 — WHERE AM I NOW?

This is a good time for self-reflection, evaluation and taking inventory.

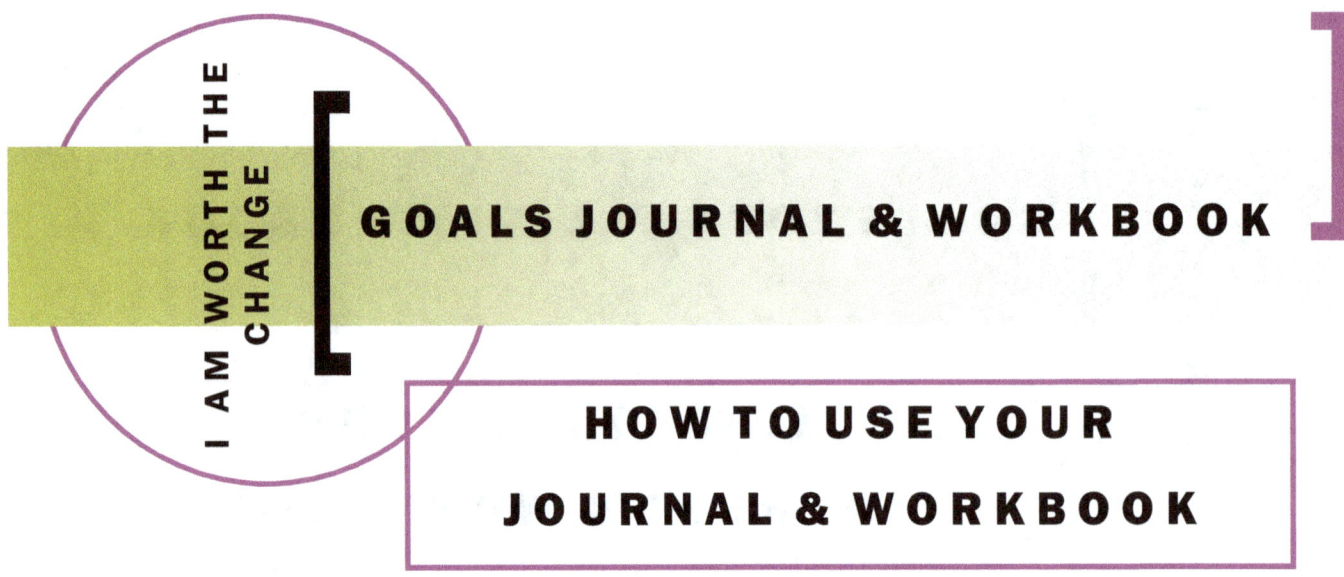

HOW TO USE YOUR JOURNAL & WORKBOOK

Are you in a good place mentally, emotionally, spiritually? What's going on in your life at this present time? What's influencing the way you think or the decisions you make? Who's in your life right now? Who are the closest people to you that your decisions might impact or who might impact your decisions?

Have you ever looked back to a time in your past and wondered how you actually felt in the moment, in light of what took place? Well, here in your journal and workbook, you get to record where you are now in your life as you set your goals. When you look back at your journal in 5 years or maybe 20 years, you'll get to read exactly what was going on. Your response to this section, will also help you to answer the next section too, "Check In: How Am I Feeling?"

Further, when considering where you are now, ask yourself: "Does my lifestyle, habits and character align with where I want to go and what I want to do?"

For instance, reaching your goals and achieving success requires consistency and discipline to name a couple. Are you disciplined? Are you consistent? Do you give up when things get hard? Do you not show up simply because you don't feel like it, even after you committed? Do you procrastinate? Are you always late? Do you overspend?

Achieving your goals is just as much about "being" the person as it is about "doing" the things.

And hey...no sweat if you're not there yet. This is the blessing of self-reflection and evaluation, to identify where growth is needed. You get to practice being who you want and need to be little by little...being disciplined, being dependable, being a good steward over your finances, health, marriage, children, business, etc. Before you know it, it's who you are!

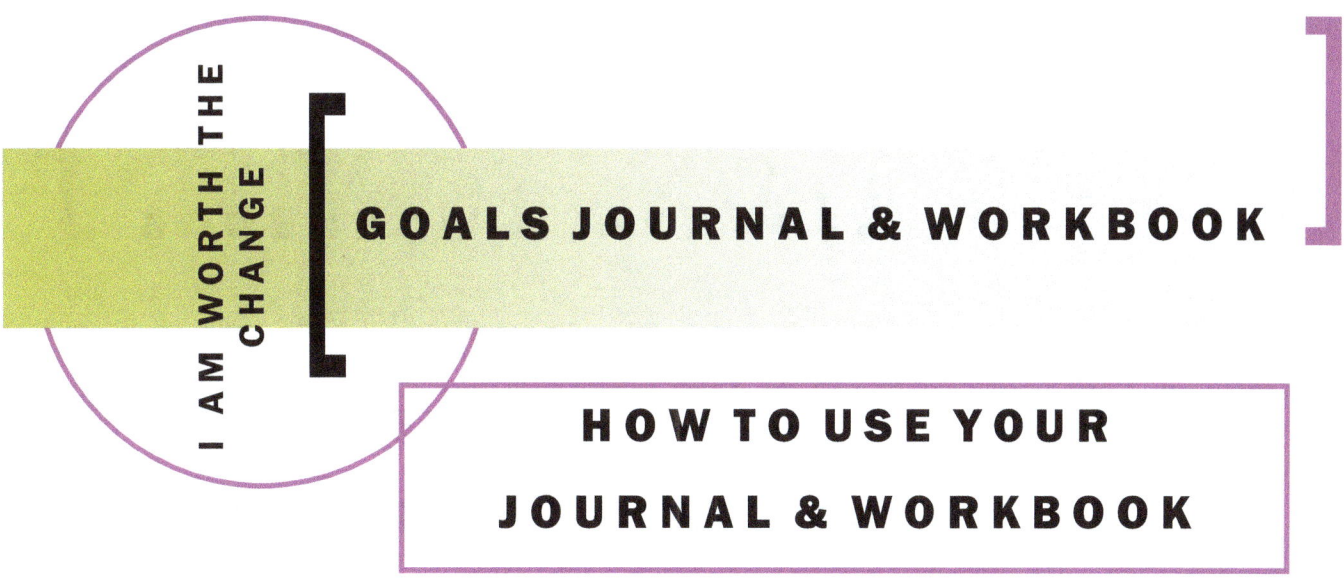

GOALS JOURNAL & WORKBOOK

HOW TO USE YOUR JOURNAL & WORKBOOK

6 — CHECK IN: HOW AM I FEELING?

I created an emotions list in the back to assist you with this. I totally get it, sometimes in the moment, it might be difficult to identify exactly how you feel. This can be due to denial or simply not wanting to face or admit how you feel, not wanting to deal with it or just uncertainty.

As you go through the list, be brave and courageous. If it fits, record it. Don't let embarrassment, guilt, shame or anything else stop you from getting breakthrough. Remember, you are not the only one who've felt these emotions and you certainly won't be the last. There are many others experiencing what you are right now. There will be some good emotions and some that are not so good, but the good news is, it's temporary. Change is coming for you.

7 — WHAT WILL THIS CHANGE DO FOR ME?

Remember, this can be connected to your "Why," the heart of your goal.

Be as detailed and specific as possible because this will serve to encourage you as you go through the process of a goal set to a goal met. You may want to revisit this space just to remind yourself of why you set the goal.

8 — WHAT ARE THE CHALLENGES I MIGHT FACE?

This is your opportunity to identify challenges that may deter, delay or derail you.

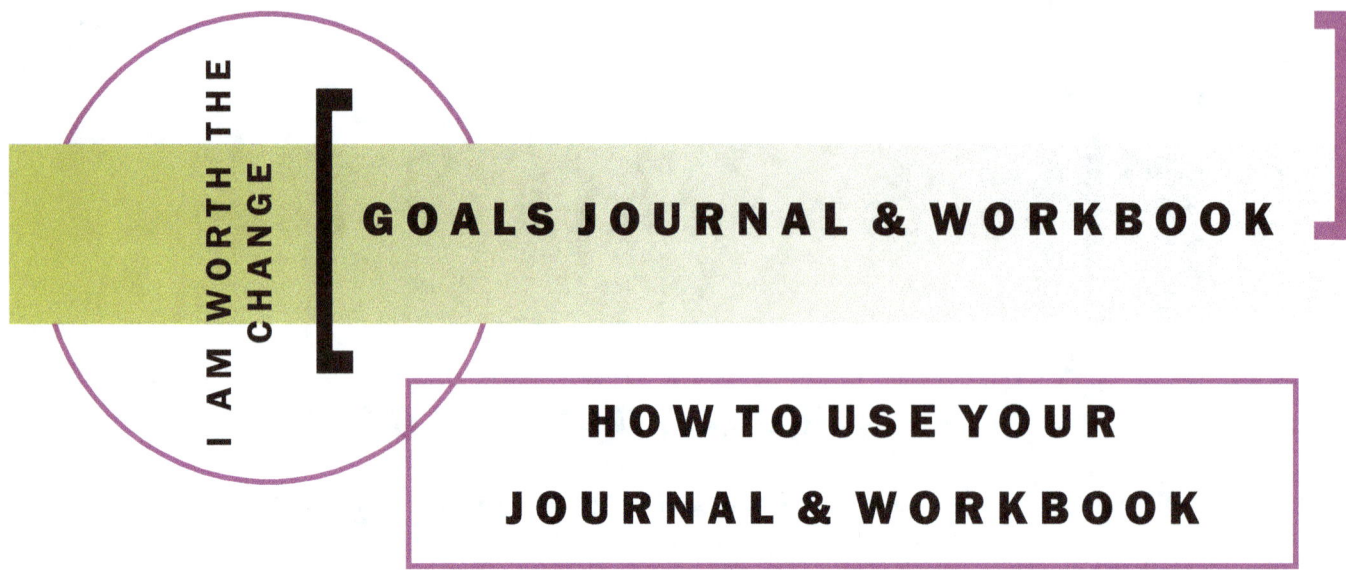

GOALS JOURNAL & WORKBOOK

HOW TO USE YOUR JOURNAL & WORKBOOK

Early recognition can prepare and position you to not make the same mistakes you used to make or to give up in the same way or at the same part of the process you used to.

You know yourself, your fears, insecurities, struggles, past, people in your life and what has the potential to set you back.

Be strong and just list the challenges, as many as you can think of and record them in this section.

9 — HOW WILL I OVERCOME THESE CHALLENGES?

Good job on being honest and listing all the possible challenges in the previous section. Now you get to do some pre-work. I call it pre-work, because how you prepare in advance before a storm, may be the very thing that saves you. If the storm passes over, yippee, but if it hits, you will be ready!

For each challenge, I want you to come up with a plan of action to overcome. Just so you know, you don't have to do this alone, you can get help and reinforcement. Your responses here may also be useful for the next section, "Do I Need Help? Do I Need Accountability?"

Some of your challenges will be internal and some external as we've previously discussed.

For instance, if you know you may feel the fear and the accusation, "who do you think you are to do this?" then get ready with your response. Your response may include affirmations and declarations that you can stand on such as: "I am chosen and created for this and I will not bow down to fear or intimidation! I am more than enough and I am capable!"

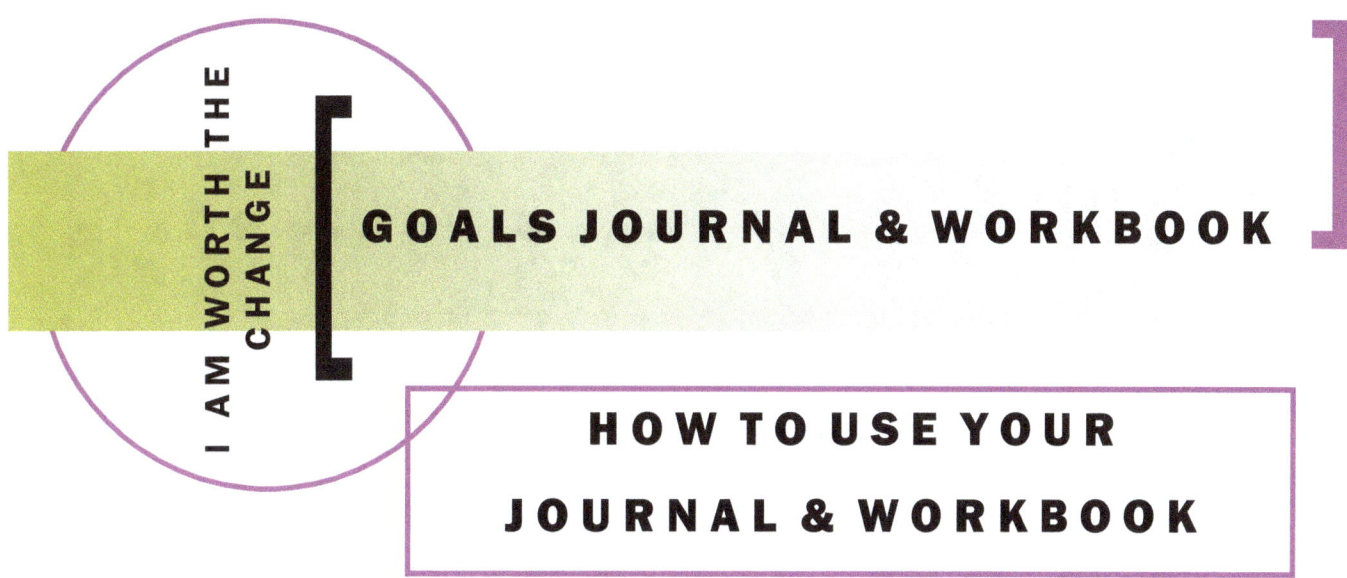

HOW TO USE YOUR JOURNAL & WORKBOOK

Be sure to write your affirmations and declarations in the section called, "My Inspiration." There is space created for them.

Another instance may be finances and you might need a certain amount of money to reach your goal. In this section, you can come up with ways to earn extra money.

Don't be discouraged by the challenges you face. Challenges create perseverance. You will discover a strength and a tenacity you didn't know you possessed. You will overcome!

10 · DO I NEED HELP? DO I NEED ACCOUNTABILITY?

Recognize your need for help. This is critical and has gotten in the way of the success of many who were determined to do it alone. Oftentimes, the dreams in our hearts are bigger than we realize. Well, some of you know this, that's why you were afraid to move forward. It's ok to get help. It's not weakness; it's wisdom!

What kind of help do you need? Write it down in this section. What kind of help would be most beneficial to you? I know—you don't want just anybody touching your dream, but the right help can make it better, stronger and more impactful.

For instance, I received the help of a book cover professional for this journal and my other books because my artistic abilities fall short of creating a look that would capture what I desire to display as the face of my work.

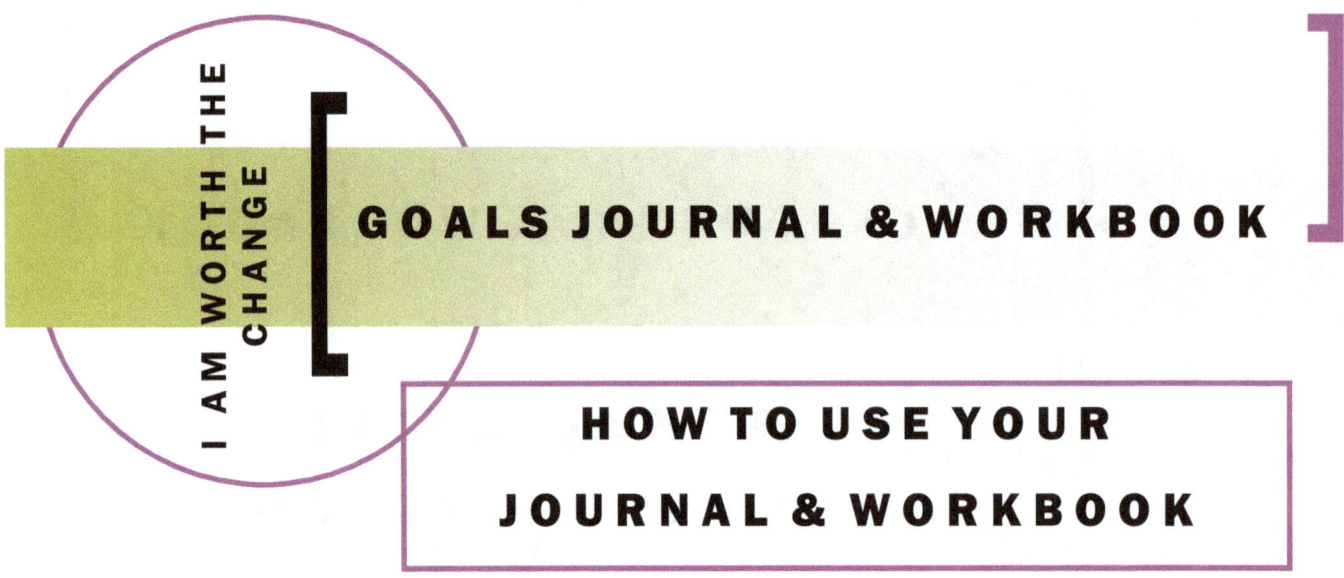

HOW TO USE YOUR JOURNAL & WORKBOOK

You can take a course to learn a new skillset. You can do online research for information you might need.

Accountability comes in many shapes and sizes. You can be part of an online support group for entrepreneurs, for divorcees, for bakers, etc. You can hire a coach or a consultant.

Be open to help and accountability, especially if you've found it difficult in times past to complete what you started or became discouraged along the way and gave up.

This section can be the game changer for you.

 LETTER OF ENCOURAGEMENT

This could be a letter, a poem, a song, a prayer, etc.

Tip #1 – If you're like most humans, you can give the best advice and encouragement to others in their time of need. So, pretend as though you are encouraging a friend who has this goal; what would you tell your friend?

Tip #2 – Share your goal with a friend or other trusted person and see what they would tell you. Write down their encouragement as part of your letter or simply use their encouragement and words as inspiration to write your letter to yourself.

Tip #3 – Sometimes, the best encouragement can come from a stranger, someone who doesn't

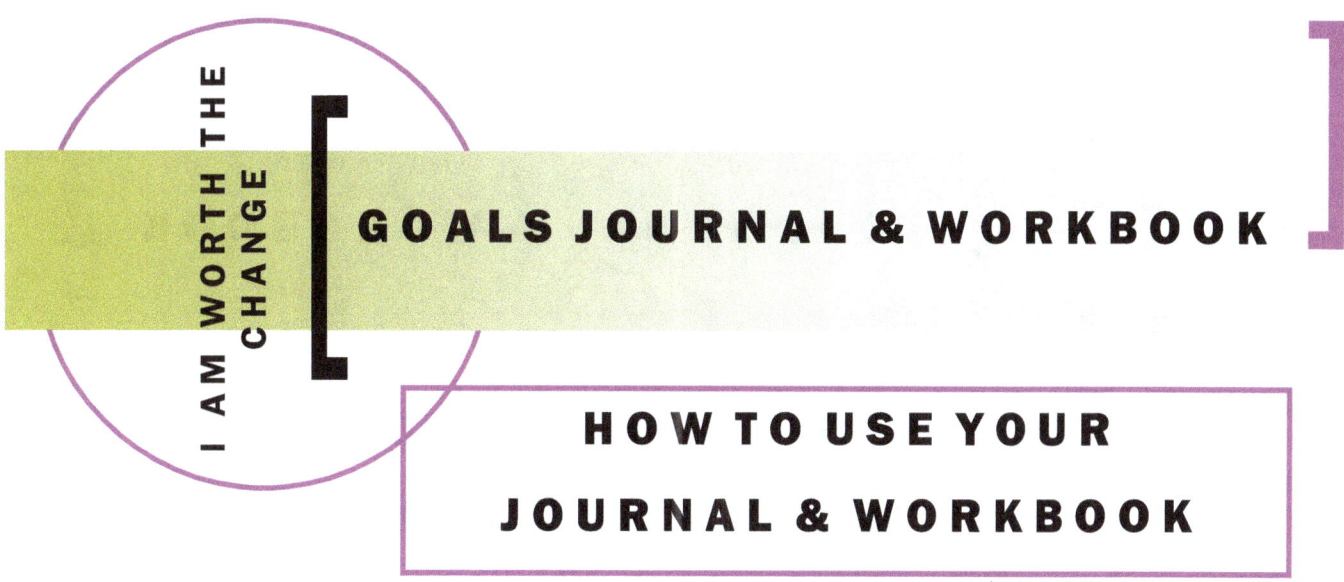

GOALS JOURNAL & WORKBOOK

HOW TO USE YOUR JOURNAL & WORKBOOK

know anything about you. You can share your goal with a stranger and be surprised at the wisdom and comfort you might receive. This "stranger" can be in one of the new groups you participate in for help, support, encouragement or accountability.

12 — MY TASK TRACKER

There is a tracking sheet for each of your goals. Identify what needs to be done for each goal you set. List them in your tracker and record the date you begin the task, set the date the task is due and make important notes for each.

Setting due dates helps to avoid procrastination. You don't have to put off until tomorrow the things that can be done today. This can bring such peace and a sense of accomplishment.

When what should've been done yesterday collides with the unexpected of today, things can be very frustrating, especially when there's consequences to putting things off. Go for balance. Don't be too hard on yourself—that can create stress and anxiety. You have wisdom. You are able to make good decisions. These are *your* goals. You set the pace.

The notes you make can be accounts you set up, important websites, names of people to follow up with, etc.

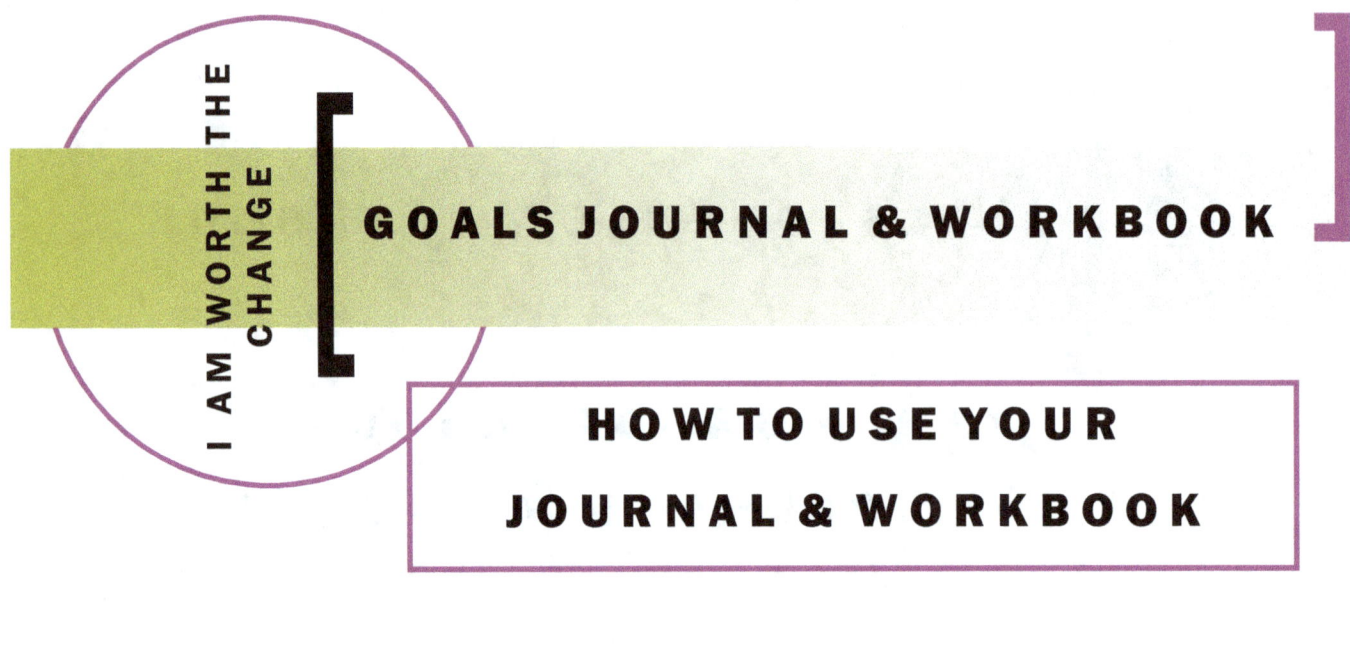

GOALS JOURNAL & WORKBOOK

HOW TO USE YOUR JOURNAL & WORKBOOK

13 — MY INSPIRATION

Here is your extra dose of motivation. This is another space to be your own greatest cheerleader.

Take it seriously and make the most of it. If a particular inspiration doesn't suit you, scratch it out and make it your own. There is room for your favorite Scripture specific to the goal you set, a quote that lights a fire under you, an affirmation that speaks to your heart about who you are and what you are able to do and a declaration for you to proclaim from your own mouth.

14 — MY RESULTS!

I like results. This page shows that YOU TRIED. You attempted something. You stepped up. You pushed and challenged yourself. You went for it. I want to tell you congratulations in advance. No matter what the results are, you can celebrate for completing your goal, valuing the lessons you learned on the journey and recognizing and embracing any adjustments that may need to be made. Be kind to yourself. If more time is needed, give yourself more time, but don't give up.

15 — CHECK IN: HOW AM I FEELING?

After it's all said and done, how you feel can be totally different than when you started. Checking in can be of vital importance. Stay in touch with how you feel, not so that your emotions can lead you, but so that they won't overtake you.

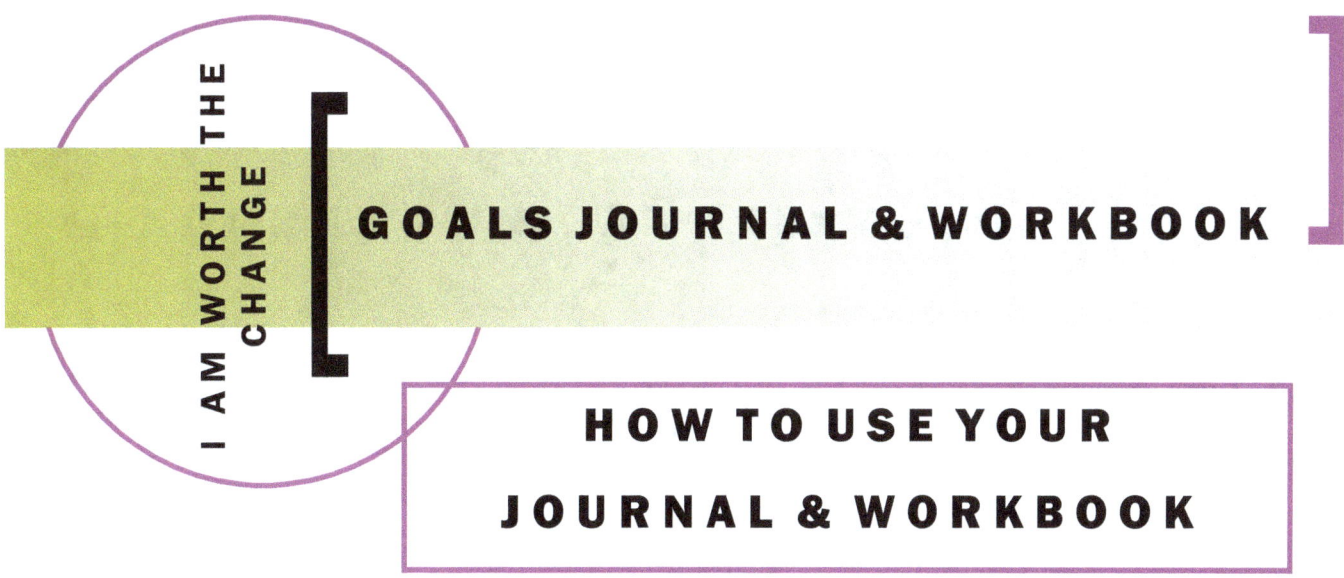

HOW TO USE YOUR JOURNAL & WORKBOOK

Again, you can use the emotions guide to assist you. Record how you feel now that you have done all the work and your results are in.

16 — **LESSONS I LEARNED**

This is the last portion of your results page, but certainly not the least. The lessons you learned are just as important as the goal you set. Some may argue that it could be even more important. You already identified how you feel at this point, but now I want you to take a deep breath and really focus on what you learned. Don't cheat yourself.

What did you learn about *you*?

What life lessons did you learn?

What did you discover along the way?

The win is great, but if you didn't quite complete it yet, that's ok too. Not to be cheesy, but this is not the space for sour lemons. So I challenge you to take every lemon, squeeze and add sugar. This is an opportunity for you to see the bright side of things. Chin up. Shoulders squared. You are amazing for what you set out to accomplish.

INTRODUCTION

Welcome to CHANGE!

Get excited! Get very excited! Don't hold back, don't look around, don't worry about who might see you or what they might have to say. YOU deserve this!

It's not just time—it's YOUR time!

What will you do with it? What will you make of it? What will you create? What will you build? What will you start? What will you open? What will you accomplish?

There are hidden treasures—opportunities—chances all around you, big and small, just waiting for you to see them and pick them up. They are waiting for your special touch to bring them to life—waiting for the heart that you have, the compassion, the hope, the vision, the wisdom, the ideas, the skills, the gifts, the talents, the leadership and the love that only YOU can bring.

Oftentimes, the hidden treasures are hidden in you. Sometimes they are covered up in fears, insecurities, painful past experiences, broken hearts and discouragement, but there is always hope and a new day, beautifully wrapped in a gift called CHANGE.

It's time to open your gift!

You are worth the CHANGE!

C.H.A.N.G.E. - Chances Happen Anytime New Goals Emerge!

INTRODUCTION

There are chances and opportunities assigned to the goals that YOU CREATE—the goals that YOU SET—the goals that YOU GO AFTER!

Open your eyes! Open your heart! Step into a whole new world of possibilities—reach out and grab them and you won't leave empty handed!

Are you ready?

Let's go!

I AM WORTH THE CHANGE

Do you hear the call?

You know what I'm talking about. It's not an external call—it's internal—calling deep from within—and it's both loud and a whisper at the same time.

> "A vision is not just a picture of what could be; it is an appeal to our better selves, a call to become something more."
> — Rosabeth Moss Kanter

For so many, the cares of life, the traumas, the fears, the insecurities, the doubts, the past, the challenges, the obstacles, have all played a part in attempting to suppress, to quiet, to hide, to ignore and to cover up the deepest parts of who you really are—the truth of who you are—your gifts, skills, talents, anointings, strengths, passions, desires, hopes and dreams—those things that make you really come alive.

It's your best you calling out—wanting to make your mark in the world—wanting to do the great things that deep down you know are possible, but have yet to explore the possibilities of them. The greatness in you has yet to be fully acknowledged, fully embraced and fully celebrated. Today, we celebrate YOU!

Now is the time! Now is your time! Now is your chance! Will you make the choice?

YOU ARE WORTH THE CHANGE!

GOALS JOURNAL & WORKBOOK

I AM WORTH THE CHANGE

VISION STATEMENT

I AM WORTH THE CHANGE

Sometimes the temporary pain and loss we experience literally does cause all things to work together for our good.

Some people have suffered the pain of a job loss, only to find that if they hadn't lost the job, they wouldn't be where they are today—some place different, some place better, some with their own thriving businesses, ministries or organizations.

Some people have suffered the loss of a relationship, only to find that they wouldn't have let go themselves, but because of the loss, they were able to experience what love really is.

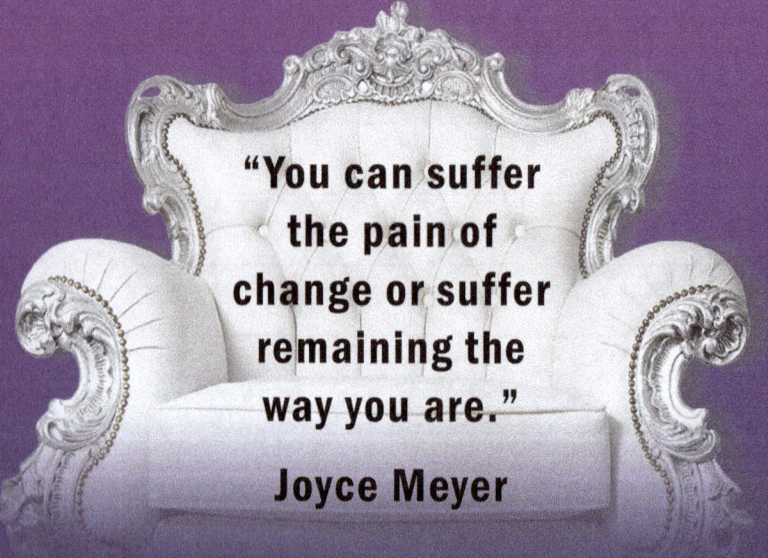

"You can suffer the pain of change or suffer remaining the way you are."
— Joyce Meyer

Some people won't choose something different or better because they are too comfortable with what they know.

The pain of change could be starting over, new people, new places, new responsibilities, new opportunities—all of which can stir up insecurities, fear of rejection, fear of being misunderstood, fear of being alone, etc.

However, for many, you have come to a place where the pain of remaining the way you are, with all the fears, the prisons of limiting beliefs, the same-old-same-old, has you ready to break free!

It's time to stretch! Come out of your comfort zone! Come out of the box! It's time to experience something completely new! It's time for change! You are worth it!

GOALS JOURNAL & WORKBOOK

GOAL:

SET DATE:

GOAL TERM:

☐ SHORT ☐ LONG

TO BE COMPLETED BY:

WHAT DO I NEED TO GET STARTED?

☐ _____
☐ _____
☐ _____
☐ _____
☐ _____
☐ _____

WHAT'S MY PLAN?

_____
_____
_____
_____
_____

GOAL #1

[**GOAL:**]

WHERE AM I NOW?

_____
_____
_____
_____
_____
_____
_____

[CHECK IN]: HOW AM I FEELING?

_____
_____
_____
_____
_____
_____
_____

WHAT WILL THIS CHANGE DO FOR ME?

_____
_____
_____
_____
_____
_____
_____

GOAL:

GOALS JOURNAL & WORKBOOK

WHAT ARE THE CHALLENGES I MIGHT FACE?

_____
_____
_____
_____
_____
_____
_____
_____

HOW WILL I OVERCOME THESE CHALLENGES?

_____
_____
_____
_____
_____
_____
_____
_____

DO I NEED HELP? DO I NEED ACCOUNTABILITY?

_____
_____
_____
_____
_____
_____
_____
_____

[**GOAL:**

WRITE YOURSELF A LETTER OF ENCOURAGEMENT

GOALS JOURNAL & WORKBOOK

TASK TRACKER

#	TASK:	START DATE: DUE DATE:	NOTES:
1.			
2.			
3.			
4.			
5.			
6.			

MY INSPIRATION

SCRIPTURE:

_____
_____
_____
_____

QUOTE:

_____
_____
_____
_____

AFFIRMATION:

_____
_____
_____
_____

DECLARATION:

_____
_____
_____
_____

GOALS JOURNAL & WORKBOOK

JOURNAL SPACE

I AM WORTH THE CHANGE

Results:

GOAL:

SET DATE:

☐ I MADE IT! LET'S CELEBRATE!

☐ I JUST NEED A LITTLE MORE TIME AND I GOT THIS!

☐ THIS IS NO LONGER A GOAL

[CHECK IN]: HOW AM I FEELING?

_____
_____
_____
_____

LESSONS I LEARNED:

1. _____
2. _____
3. _____

WHAT DO I NEED TO GET TO THE FINISHED LINE?

☐ _____
☐ _____
☐ _____

I AM WORTH THE CHANGE

Do you lack courage?

When you lack courage, you shrink back in fear imagining all the "what-ifs."

Have you ever become upset or frustrated because you wanted to do something you didn't have the courage to do?

"Finding the courage to do what you never thought you could is a treasure that never stops rewarding you."

Floydise Paquette

Courage can catapult you into the pursuit of greatness!

Courage is not a one-off tool that you take out of the box and put it back. Courage is a treasure that once you find it, it continues to work for you, bringing you into new places and opening up gifts on the inside of you that you never knew were there. It's a never-ending resource that shows up to face even the greatest of giants, your biggest critics and your worst enemies. It doesn't back down!

Courage moves forward despite the opposition.

Courage sees "No" on a door and goes to knock on another one.

Have you found courage? It's not a tool, it's a treasure! It will change your life!

YOU ARE WORTH THE CHANGE!

GOAL:

SET DATE:

GOALS JOURNAL & WORKBOOK

GOAL TERM:

☐ SHORT ☐ LONG

TO BE COMPLETED BY:

WHAT DO I NEED TO GET STARTED?

☐ _____
☐ _____
☐ _____
☐ _____
☐ _____
☐ _____

WHAT'S MY PLAN?

_____
_____
_____
_____
_____

GOAL #2

[**GOAL:**]

WHERE AM I NOW?

_____
_____
_____
_____
_____
_____
_____

[CHECK IN]: HOW AM I FEELING?

_____
_____
_____
_____
_____
_____
_____

WHAT WILL THIS CHANGE DO FOR ME?

_____
_____
_____
_____
_____
_____
_____

WHAT ARE THE CHALLENGES I MIGHT FACE?

___

HOW WILL I OVERCOME THESE CHALLENGES?

___

DO I NEED HELP? DO I NEED ACCOUNTABILITY?

___

GOAL:

WRITE YOURSELF A LETTER OF ENCOURAGEMENT

TASK TRACKER

#	TASK:	START DATE: DUE DATE:	NOTES:
1.			
2.			
3.			
4.			
5.			
6.			

MY INSPIRATION

SCRIPTURE:

_____
_____
_____
_____

QUOTE:

_____
_____
_____
_____

AFFIRMATION:

_____
_____
_____
_____

DECLARATION:

_____
_____
_____
_____

GOALS JOURNAL & WORKBOOK

I AM WORTH THE CHANGE

JOURNAL SPACE

I AM WORTH THE CHANGE

Results:

GOAL:

SET DATE:

○ I MADE IT! LET'S CELEBRATE! ☐

○ I JUST NEED A LITTLE MORE TIME AND I GOT THIS! ☐

○ THIS IS NO LONGER A GOAL ☐

[CHECK IN]: HOW AM I FEELING?

_____
_____
_____
_____

LESSONS I LEARNED:

1. _____
2. _____
3. _____

WHAT DO I NEED TO GET TO THE FINISHED LINE?

☐ _____
☐ _____
☐ _____

Page 42

I AM WORTH THE CHANGE

You're Up! It's Your Time! It's Your Turn!

It is over for everything that has kept you benched and on the sidelines watching others hit it out of the park in life.

Intimidation—your time is up!

People-pleasing—your time is up!

Guilt—your time is up!

Manipulation—your time is up!

Fear—your time is up!

Shame—your time is up!

Unworthiness—your time is up!

Right now—it is your moment!

> "Never let the fear of striking out keep you from playing the game."
> **Babe Ruth**

DO NOT FEAR STRIKING OUT!

GET UP!

STEP UP TO THE PLATE AND GIVE IT ALL YOU'VE GOT!

YOU ARE ENOUGH! I don't care what people said to you in the past. I don't care about what they will say or think. I cast every negative word to the ground—they will no longer hold you down!

GET UP! YOU ARE ENOUGH! GO FOR IT!

GOALS JOURNAL & WORKBOOK

I AM WORTH THE CHANGE

GOAL:

SET DATE:

GOAL TERM:

☐ SHORT ☐ LONG

TO BE COMPLETED BY:

WHAT DO I NEED TO GET STARTED?

☐ _____
☐ _____
☐ _____
☐ _____
☐ _____
☐ _____

WHAT'S MY PLAN?

_____
_____
_____
_____
_____

GOAL #3

[**GOAL:**]

WHERE AM I NOW?

_____
_____
_____
_____
_____
_____
_____

[CHECK IN]: HOW AM I FEELING?

_____
_____
_____
_____
_____
_____
_____

WHAT WILL THIS CHANGE DO FOR ME?

_____
_____
_____
_____
_____
_____
_____

GOALS JOURNAL & WORKBOOK

WHAT ARE THE CHALLENGES I MIGHT FACE?

_____
_____
_____
_____
_____
_____
_____
_____

HOW WILL I OVERCOME THESE CHALLENGES?

_____
_____
_____
_____
_____
_____
_____
_____

DO I NEED HELP? DO I NEED ACCOUNTABILITY?

_____
_____
_____
_____
_____
_____
_____
_____

[**GOAL:**]

WRITE YOURSELF A LETTER OF ENCOURAGEMENT

TASK TRACKER

#	TASK:	START DATE: DUE DATE:	NOTES:
1.			
2.			
3.			
4.			
5.			
6.			

GOALS JOURNAL & WORKBOOK

MY INSPIRATION

SCRIPTURE:

_____
_____
_____
_____

QUOTE:

_____
_____
_____
_____

AFFIRMATION:

_____
_____
_____
_____

DECLARATION:

_____
_____
_____
_____

GOALS JOURNAL & WORKBOOK

JOURNAL SPACE

I AM WORTH THE CHANGE

Results:

GOAL:

SET DATE:

○ I MADE IT! LET'S CELEBRATE!

○ I JUST NEED A LITTLE MORE TIME AND I GOT THIS!

○ THIS IS NO LONGER A GOAL

[CHECK IN]: HOW AM I FEELING?

_____
_____
_____
_____

LESSONS I LEARNED:

1.
2.
3.

WHAT DO I NEED TO GET TO THE FINISHED LINE?

☐
☐
☐

I AM WORTH THE CHANGE

How are you measuring your success?

Comparison has been an effective tool that has caused a countless number of people to draw the conclusion they are inadequate—they don't have what it takes.

They look at what others have done or are doing and say, "How can I compare to that?" Sometimes, we look at what others are doing and determine that nothing else needs to be done. It looks as though they have already done it all and so you count yourself out. You discount what you have and what you have to say. You discount your dream, your vision, your gift, your contribution and you become discouraged.

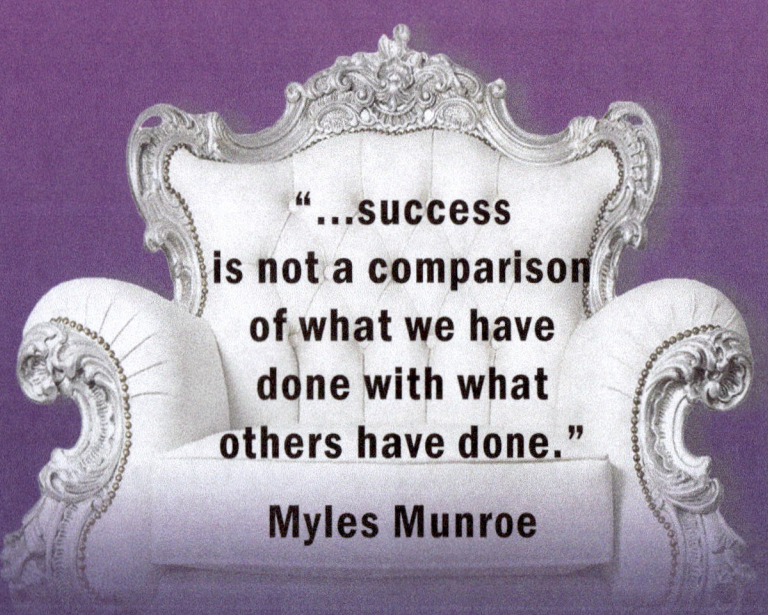

"...success is not a comparison of what we have done with what others have done."

Myles Munroe

Your vision is a unique blueprint for your success. Your vision can become obscured when you watch what others are doing and compare. You cannot build with blurred vision.

It's time to refocus. Keep your eyes on your own work.

You are not trying to *become* a success, you are a success causing your vision to become a reality!

YOU ARE WORTH THE CHANGE!

GOALS JOURNAL & WORKBOOK

I AM WORTH THE CHANGE

GOAL:

SET DATE:

GOAL TERM:

☐ SHORT   ☐ LONG

TO BE COMPLETED BY:

WHAT DO I NEED TO GET STARTED?

☐ _____
☐ _____
☐ _____
☐ _____
☐ _____
☐ _____

WHAT'S MY PLAN?

_____
_____
_____
_____
_____

GOAL #4

[**GOAL:**]

WHERE AM I NOW?

_____
_____
_____
_____
_____
_____
_____

[CHECK IN]: HOW AM I FEELING?

_____
_____
_____
_____
_____
_____
_____

WHAT WILL THIS CHANGE DO FOR ME?

_____
_____
_____
_____
_____
_____
_____

GOALS JOURNAL & WORKBOOK

Page 57

WHAT ARE THE CHALLENGES I MIGHT FACE?

___

HOW WILL I OVERCOME THESE CHALLENGES?

___

DO I NEED HELP? DO I NEED ACCOUNTABILITY?

___

[**GOAL:**]

WRITE YOURSELF A LETTER OF ENCOURAGEMENT

GOALS JOURNAL & WORKBOOK

TASK TRACKER

#	TASK:	START DATE: DUE DATE:	NOTES:
1.			
2.			
3.			
4.			
5.			
6.			

MY INSPIRATION

SCRIPTURE:

_____
_____
_____
_____

QUOTE:

_____
_____
_____
_____

AFFIRMATION:

_____
_____
_____
_____

DECLARATION:

_____
_____
_____
_____

GOALS JOURNAL & WORKBOOK

JOURNAL SPACE

_____
_____
_____
_____
_____
_____
_____
_____
_____
_____
_____
_____
_____
_____
_____
_____
_____
_____
_____
_____

I AM WORTH THE CHANGE

I AM WORTH THE CHANGE

Results:

GOAL:

SET DATE:

○ I MADE IT! LET'S CELEBRATE! ☐

○ I JUST NEED A LITTLE MORE TIME AND I GOT THIS! ☐

○ THIS IS NO LONGER A GOAL ☐

[CHECK IN]: HOW AM I FEELING?

_____
_____
_____
_____

LESSONS I LEARNED:

1. _____
2. _____
3. _____

WHAT DO I NEED TO GET TO THE FINISHED LINE?

☐ _____
☐ _____
☐ _____

I AM WORTH THE CHANGE

Have you ever heard of Imposter Syndrome?

I heard someone say, imposter syndrome is when you are connecting to the old you and not who you are now or who you're becoming.

Who are you? You need to know who you are just as sure as you know your name. When someone asks your name, you state it emphatically, with no doubt or reservation.

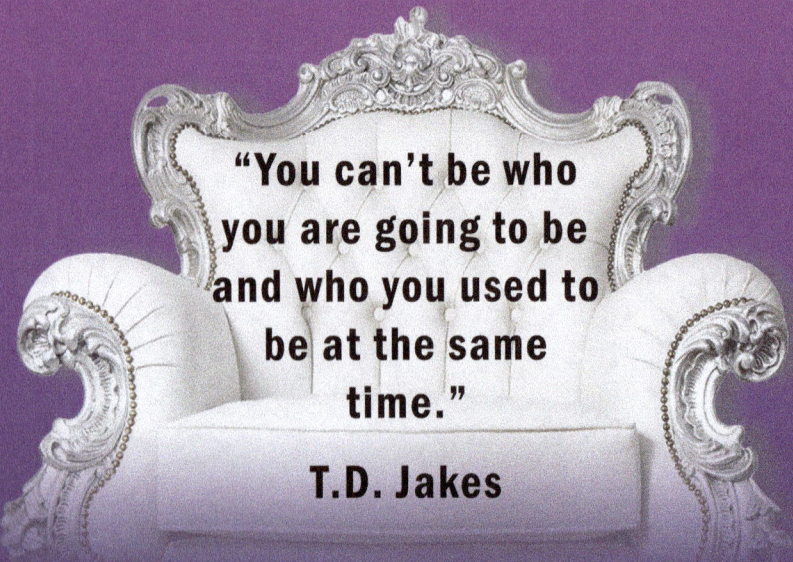

"You can't be who you are going to be and who you used to be at the same time."
T.D. Jakes

Who you are needs to be just as clear.

You are not your past. You are not your mistakes.

Imposter syndrome questions, "Who am I to do this?" "Who do you think you are?"

You fear that others will have the same accusations against you and reject you. You feel like you are a hypocrite and pretending to be someone or something you're not.

It's all lies. It's you identifying with the old you that you have already disqualified.

You are not pretending to be great; it's who you are! The old you just didn't know it. Now, you know it! Your loyalty is not to who you used to be, it's to who you really are.

YOU ARE WORTH THE CHANGE!

GOALS JOURNAL & WORKBOOK

I AM WORTH THE CHANGE

GOAL:

SET DATE:

GOAL TERM:

☐ SHORT   ☐ LONG

TO BE COMPLETED BY:

WHAT DO I NEED TO GET STARTED?

☐ _____
☐ _____
☐ _____
☐ _____
☐ _____
☐ _____

WHAT'S MY PLAN?

_____
_____
_____
_____
_____

GOAL #5

Page 65

[**GOAL:**]

WHERE AM I NOW?

_____
_____
_____
_____
_____
_____
_____

[CHECK IN]: HOW AM I FEELING?

_____
_____
_____
_____
_____
_____
_____

WHAT WILL THIS CHANGE DO FOR ME?

_____
_____
_____
_____
_____
_____
_____

GOALS JOURNAL & WORKBOOK

WHAT ARE THE CHALLENGES I MIGHT FACE?

_____
_____
_____
_____
_____
_____
_____
_____

HOW WILL I OVERCOME THESE CHALLENGES?

_____
_____
_____
_____
_____
_____
_____
_____

DO I NEED HELP? DO I NEED ACCOUNTABILITY?

_____
_____
_____
_____
_____
_____
_____
_____

GOAL:

WRITE YOURSELF A LETTER OF ENCOURAGEMENT

GOALS JOURNAL & WORKBOOK

TASK TRACKER

#	TASK:	START DATE: DUE DATE:	NOTES:
1.			
2.			
3.			
4.			
5.			
6.			

GOALS JOURNAL & WORKBOOK

MY INSPIRATION

SCRIPTURE:

___

QUOTE:

___

AFFIRMATION:

___

DECLARATION:

___

GOALS JOURNAL & WORKBOOK

I AM WORTH THE CHANGE

JOURNAL SPACE

_____
_____
_____
_____
_____
_____
_____
_____
_____
_____
_____
_____
_____
_____
_____
_____
_____
_____
_____
_____

I AM WORTH THE CHANGE

Results:

GOAL:

SET DATE:

○ I MADE IT! LET'S CELEBRATE!

○ I JUST NEED A LITTLE MORE TIME AND I GOT THIS!

○ THIS IS NO LONGER A GOAL

[CHECK IN]: HOW AM I FEELING?

_____
_____
_____
_____

LESSONS I LEARNED:

1.
2.
3.

WHAT DO I NEED TO GET TO THE FINISHED LINE?

☐
☐
☐

I AM WORTH THE CHANGE

One of the questions in this journal is, "What will this change do for me?" In this journal, you've been identifying obstacles and overcoming them.

When you achieve a goal, something not only happens on the outside, but there is a change that happens on the inside.

"What you get by achieving your goals is not as important as what you become by achieving your goals."

Zig Ziglar

When you make it through years of school or a program, when you make it through a trial or a tough time, when you overcome sickness, when you overcome difficulty in a marriage or with your children, when you overcome attacks from your enemies, you are no longer who you *were* on the other side of it.

Change took place. There was growth, mentally, emotionally, spiritually, relationally, financially, etc.

You conquered things you were once afraid to even face. You got up when you were knocked down. You stayed in the race even when you felt like giving up.

It's not just about the goals. It's about the change that occurs in the midst of them. The change that takes place *in you*!

YOU ARE WORTH THE CHANGE!

GOALS JOURNAL & WORKBOOK

GOAL:

SET DATE:

GOAL TERM:

☐ SHORT   ☐ LONG

TO BE COMPLETED BY:

WHAT DO I NEED TO GET STARTED?

☐ _____
☐ _____
☐ _____
☐ _____
☐ _____
☐ _____

WHAT'S MY PLAN?

_____
_____
_____
_____
_____

[**GOAL:**]

WHERE AM I NOW?

___

[CHECK IN]: HOW AM I FEELING?

___

WHAT WILL THIS CHANGE DO FOR ME?

___

GOALS JOURNAL & WORKBOOK

WHAT ARE THE CHALLENGES I MIGHT FACE?

_____
_____
_____
_____
_____
_____
_____
_____

HOW WILL I OVERCOME THESE CHALLENGES?

_____
_____
_____
_____
_____
_____
_____
_____

DO I NEED HELP? DO I NEED ACCOUNTABILITY?

_____
_____
_____
_____
_____
_____
_____
_____

[**GOAL:**

WRITE YOURSELF A LETTER OF ENCOURAGEMENT

GOALS JOURNAL & WORKBOOK

TASK TRACKER

#	TASK:	START DATE: DUE DATE:	NOTES:
1.			
2.			
3.			
4.			
5.			
6.			

GOALS JOURNAL & WORKBOOK

MY INSPIRATION

SCRIPTURE:

_____
_____
_____
_____

QUOTE:

_____
_____
_____
_____

AFFIRMATION:

_____
_____
_____
_____

DECLARATION:

_____
_____
_____
_____

GOALS JOURNAL & WORKBOOK

JOURNAL SPACE

I AM WORTH THE CHANGE

Results:

GOAL:

SET DATE:

◯ I MADE IT! LET'S CELEBRATE! ☐

◯ I JUST NEED A LITTLE MORE TIME AND I GOT THIS! ☐

◯ THIS IS NO LONGER A GOAL ☐

[CHECK IN]: HOW AM I FEELING?

_____
_____
_____
_____

LESSONS I LEARNED:

1.
2.
3.

WHAT DO I NEED TO GET TO THE FINISHED LINE?

☐
☐
☐

I AM WORTH THE CHANGE

One of the things you are encouraged to do in this journal is to check in—to identify how you are feeling. Your mindset—your attitude is critical.

When you check in, it requires you to be honest.

Honesty means recognizing and admitting when you are the one getting in the way of your own success.

You cannot have an attitude of defeat at the same time you are trying to win.

> "I believe it is our attitude that determines our altitude. It is our attitude that allows us to soar above those things that would otherwise overcome us."
>
> **T.D. Jakes**

Your expectation is the foundation of your game plan.

Are your expectations positive? Are your expectations favorable toward you? Do your expectations set you up for the victory or do you find yourself fighting against yourself with a negative attitude or outlook.

Check your thoughts. Check your emotions and your attitude to see if they line up with where you want to go.

What imaginations do you need to cast down? What lies do you need to challenge in order to walk in the truth?

If your own attitude keeps pulling you back down and out, it's time to check them, so that you can rise and soar!

GOALS JOURNAL & WORKBOOK

I AM WORTH THE CHANGE

GOAL:

SET DATE:

GOAL TERM:

☐ SHORT ☐ LONG

TO BE COMPLETED BY:

WHAT DO I NEED TO GET STARTED?

☐ _____
☐ _____
☐ _____
☐ _____
☐ _____
☐ _____

WHAT'S MY PLAN?

_____
_____
_____
_____
_____

[**GOAL:**]

WHERE AM I NOW?

_____
_____
_____
_____
_____
_____
_____

[CHECK IN]: HOW AM I FEELING?

_____
_____
_____
_____
_____
_____
_____

WHAT WILL THIS CHANGE DO FOR ME?

_____
_____
_____
_____
_____
_____
_____

GOALS JOURNAL & WORKBOOK

WHAT ARE THE CHALLENGES I MIGHT FACE?

_____
_____
_____
_____
_____
_____
_____
_____

HOW WILL I OVERCOME THESE CHALLENGES?

_____
_____
_____
_____
_____
_____
_____
_____

DO I NEED HELP? DO I NEED ACCOUNTABILITY?

_____
_____
_____
_____
_____
_____
_____
_____

[GOAL:]

WRITE YOURSELF A LETTER OF ENCOURAGEMENT

GOALS JOURNAL & WORKBOOK

I AM WORTH THE CHANGE

TASK TRACKER

#	TASK:	START DATE: DUE DATE:	NOTES:
1.			
2.			
3.			
4.			
5.			
6.			

MY INSPIRATION

SCRIPTURE:

_____
_____
_____
_____

QUOTE:

_____
_____
_____
_____

AFFIRMATION:

_____
_____
_____
_____

DECLARATION:

_____
_____
_____
_____

GOALS JOURNAL & WORKBOOK

I AM WORTH THE CHANGE

JOURNAL SPACE

_____
_____
_____
_____
_____
_____
_____
_____
_____
_____
_____
_____
_____
_____
_____
_____
_____
_____
_____
_____
_____
_____

Results:

I AM WORTH THE CHANGE

GOAL:

SET DATE:

○ I MADE IT! LET'S CELEBRATE!

○ I JUST NEED A LITTLE MORE TIME AND I GOT THIS!

○ THIS IS NO LONGER A GOAL

[CHECK IN]: HOW AM I FEELING?

_____
_____
_____
_____

LESSONS I LEARNED:

1.
2.
3.

WHAT DO I NEED TO GET TO THE FINISHED LINE?

☐
☐
☐

I AM WORTH THE CHANGE

Rise! I speak to every dream, hope, gift, talent, and anointing within you—RISE!

You don't have to cry anymore!

Your dream will live!

HOPE AGAIN!

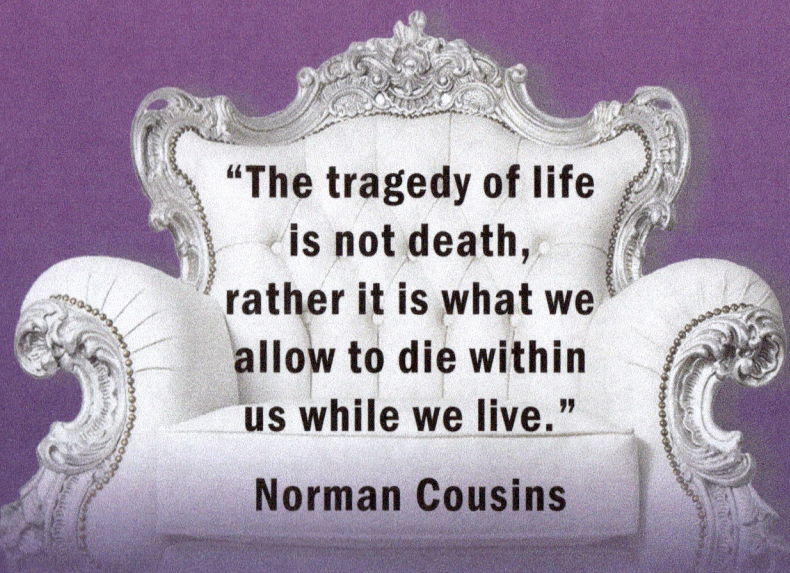

"The tragedy of life is not death, rather it is what we allow to die within us while we live."
Norman Cousins

I decree and declare that disappointment is not your portion!

It is not over for you!

It is not too late!

Don't beat yourself up another day!

Don't point fingers and don't push blame!

You will not walk in regret or resentment.

Do not look back!

Right now you are being empowered and strengthened to rise up and move forward.

Today is a new day for you! It is a fresh start and a new beginning! Take a deep breath and smell the victory! Change is in the air! You are worth it!

GOALS JOURNAL & WORKBOOK

I AM WORTH THE CHANGE

GOAL:

SET DATE:

GOAL TERM:

☐ SHORT ☐ LONG

TO BE COMPLETED BY:

WHAT DO I NEED TO GET STARTED?

☐ _____
☐ _____
☐ _____
☐ _____
☐ _____
☐ _____

WHAT'S MY PLAN?

_____
_____
_____
_____
_____

[**GOAL:**]

WHERE AM I NOW?

_____
_____
_____
_____
_____
_____
_____

[CHECK IN]: HOW AM I FEELING?

_____
_____
_____
_____
_____
_____
_____

WHAT WILL THIS CHANGE DO FOR ME?

_____
_____
_____
_____
_____
_____
_____

GOALS JOURNAL & WORKBOOK

WHAT ARE THE CHALLENGES I MIGHT FACE?

_____
_____
_____
_____
_____
_____
_____
_____

HOW WILL I OVERCOME THESE CHALLENGES?

_____
_____
_____
_____
_____
_____
_____
_____

DO I NEED HELP? DO I NEED ACCOUNTABILITY?

_____
_____
_____
_____
_____
_____
_____
_____

[**GOAL:**]

WRITE YOURSELF A LETTER OF ENCOURAGEMENT

GOALS JOURNAL & WORKBOOK

TASK TRACKER

#	TASK:	START DATE: DUE DATE:	NOTES:
1.			
2.			
3.			
4.			
5.			
6.			

GOALS JOURNAL & WORKBOOK

MY INSPIRATION

SCRIPTURE:

_____
_____
_____
_____

QUOTE:

_____
_____
_____
_____

AFFIRMATION:

_____
_____
_____
_____

DECLARATION:

_____
_____
_____
_____

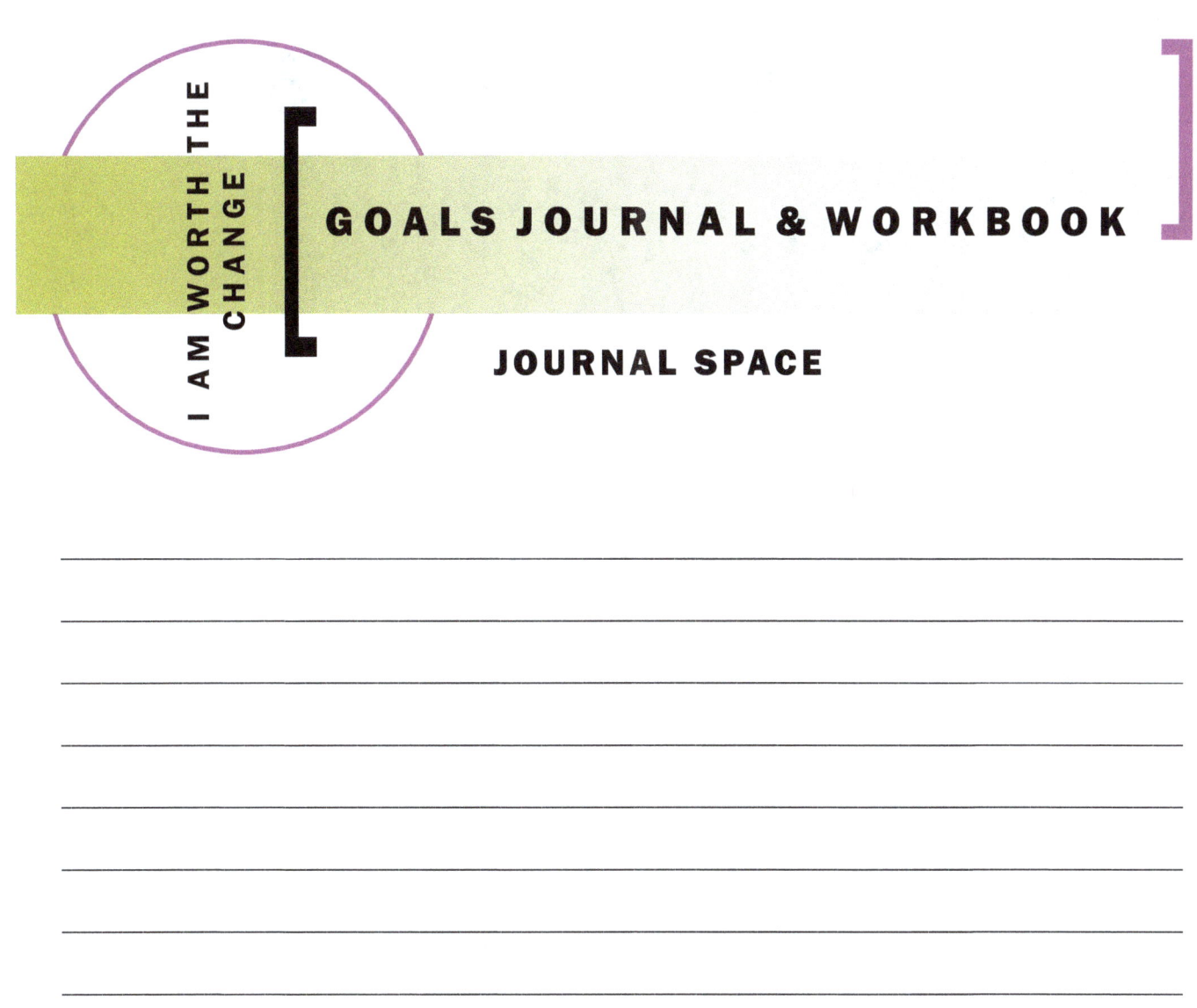

I AM WORTH THE CHANGE

Results:

GOAL:

SET DATE:

○ I MADE IT! LET'S CELEBRATE! □

○ I JUST NEED A LITTLE MORE TIME AND I GOT THIS! □

○ THIS IS NO LONGER A GOAL □

[CHECK IN]: HOW AM I FEELING?

_____
_____
_____
_____

LESSONS I LEARNED:

1. _____
2. _____
3. _____

WHAT DO I NEED TO GET TO THE FINISHED LINE?

□ _____
□ _____
□ _____

I AM WORTH THE CHANGE

What do you see?

FOCUS and look again.

What do you see?

If it's not edifying, if it doesn't build you up, if it doesn't encourage you, keep looking.

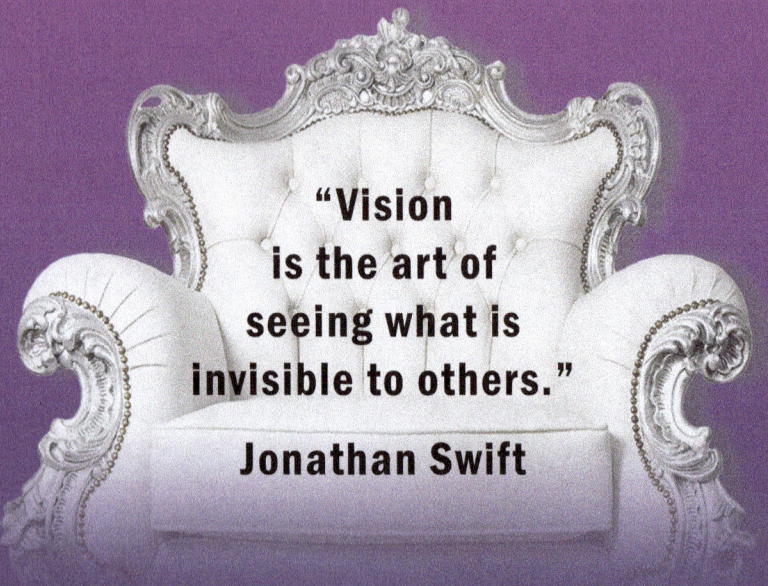

"Vision is the art of seeing what is invisible to others."
Jonathan Swift

If when you look, you see something great and hope rises and stirs within you, but then immediately after, the lies start speaking that you are not good enough, reminding you of your past or telling you all the reasons why you don't qualify, cast them down.

Vision is a gift. Sometimes it is a gift that only you get to open and no one else will see. It is divinely connected to who you are.

If you have become frustrated and discouraged by waiting for others to confirm or validate the vision in your heart, if you have doubted your dream because no one else seems to understand or support you, be encouraged!

Sometimes, in order to protect the vision, it has to be invisible to others.

Be strong and courageous and bring your vision to life!

YOU ARE WORTH THE CHANGE!

GOALS JOURNAL & WORKBOOK

I AM WORTH THE CHANGE

GOAL:

SET DATE:

GOAL TERM:

☐ SHORT   ☐ LONG

TO BE COMPLETED BY:

WHAT DO I NEED TO GET STARTED?

☐ _____
☐ _____
☐ _____
☐ _____
☐ _____
☐ _____

WHAT'S MY PLAN?

_____
_____
_____
_____
_____

GOAL #9

[**GOAL:**]

WHERE AM I NOW?

_____
_____
_____
_____
_____
_____
_____

[CHECK IN]: HOW AM I FEELING?

_____
_____
_____
_____
_____
_____
_____

WHAT WILL THIS CHANGE DO FOR ME?

_____
_____
_____
_____
_____
_____
_____

GOALS JOURNAL & WORKBOOK

WHAT ARE THE CHALLENGES I MIGHT FACE?

___

HOW WILL I OVERCOME THESE CHALLENGES?

___

DO I NEED HELP? DO I NEED ACCOUNTABILITY?

___

GOAL:

WRITE YOURSELF A LETTER OF ENCOURAGEMENT

TASK TRACKER

#	TASK:	START DATE: DUE DATE:	NOTES:
1.			
2.			
3.			
4.			
5.			
6.			

MY INSPIRATION

SCRIPTURE:

_____
_____
_____
_____

QUOTE:

_____
_____
_____
_____

AFFIRMATION:

_____
_____
_____
_____

DECLARATION:

_____
_____
_____
_____

GOALS JOURNAL & WORKBOOK

JOURNAL SPACE

_____
_____
_____
_____
_____
_____
_____
_____
_____
_____
_____
_____
_____
_____
_____
_____
_____
_____
_____
_____

Results:

I AM WORTH THE CHANGE

GOAL:

SET DATE:

○ I MADE IT! LET'S CELEBRATE!

○ I JUST NEED A LITTLE MORE TIME AND I GOT THIS!

○ THIS IS NO LONGER A GOAL

[CHECK IN]: HOW AM I FEELING?

_____
_____
_____
_____

LESSONS I LEARNED:

1. _____
2. _____
3. _____

WHAT DO I NEED TO GET TO THE FINISHED LINE?

☐ _____
☐ _____
☐ _____

I AM WORTH THE CHANGE

FREEDOM!

It's time to live! Live like it's heaven on earth—because it is!

Have you ever considered what you would do if no one was watching—if no one could judge you or criticize you?

Consider it! It's time to break off the inhibitions!

It's time to break off the chains of what people might think of you.

> "Sing like no one's listening, love like you've never been hurt, dance like nobody's watching, and live like it's heaven on earth."
>
> **Unknown**
> (Attributed to various sources)

You have ONE life to live!

BE FREE!

Some people may ask, "How can my big dreams fit into my reality?" I ask, "What if your big dreams are your reality, but you just have to CHOOSE them?"

The choice is always yours. Choose well!

See the vision, set the goal and succeed!

Sing again! Love again! Dance again! LIVE!

GO FOR IT!

YOU ARE WORTH THE CHANGE!

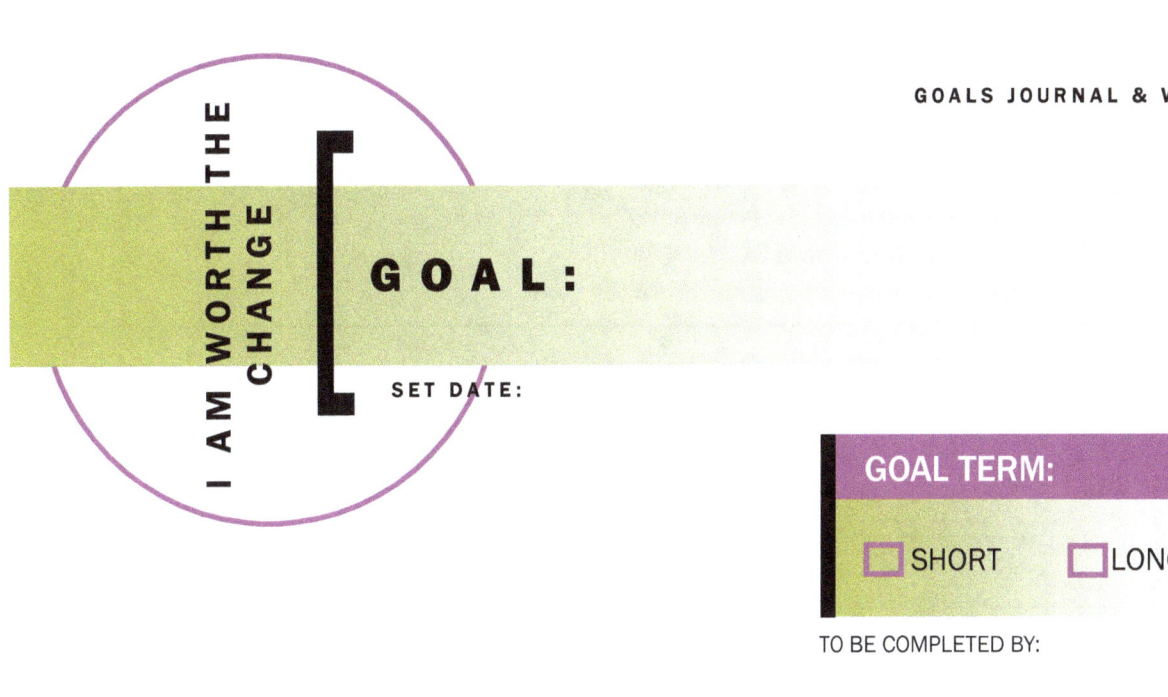

GOALS JOURNAL & WORKBOOK

I AM WORTH THE CHANGE

GOAL:

SET DATE:

GOAL TERM:

☐ SHORT ☐ LONG

TO BE COMPLETED BY:

WHAT DO I NEED TO GET STARTED?

☐ _____
☐ _____
☐ _____
☐ _____
☐ _____
☐ _____

WHAT'S MY PLAN?

_____
_____
_____
_____
_____

GOAL #10

[**GOAL:**]

WHERE AM I NOW?

[CHECK IN]: HOW AM I FEELING?

WHAT WILL THIS CHANGE DO FOR ME?

GOALS JOURNAL & WORKBOOK

WHAT ARE THE CHALLENGES I MIGHT FACE?

HOW WILL I OVERCOME THESE CHALLENGES?

DO I NEED HELP? DO I NEED ACCOUNTABILITY?

[GOAL:]

WRITE YOURSELF A LETTER OF ENCOURAGEMENT

GOALS JOURNAL & WORKBOOK

TASK TRACKER

#	TASK:	START DATE: DUE DATE:	NOTES:
1.			
2.			
3.			
4.			
5.			
6.			

MY INSPIRATION

SCRIPTURE:

_____
_____
_____
_____

QUOTE:

_____
_____
_____
_____

AFFIRMATION:

_____
_____
_____
_____

DECLARATION:

_____
_____
_____
_____

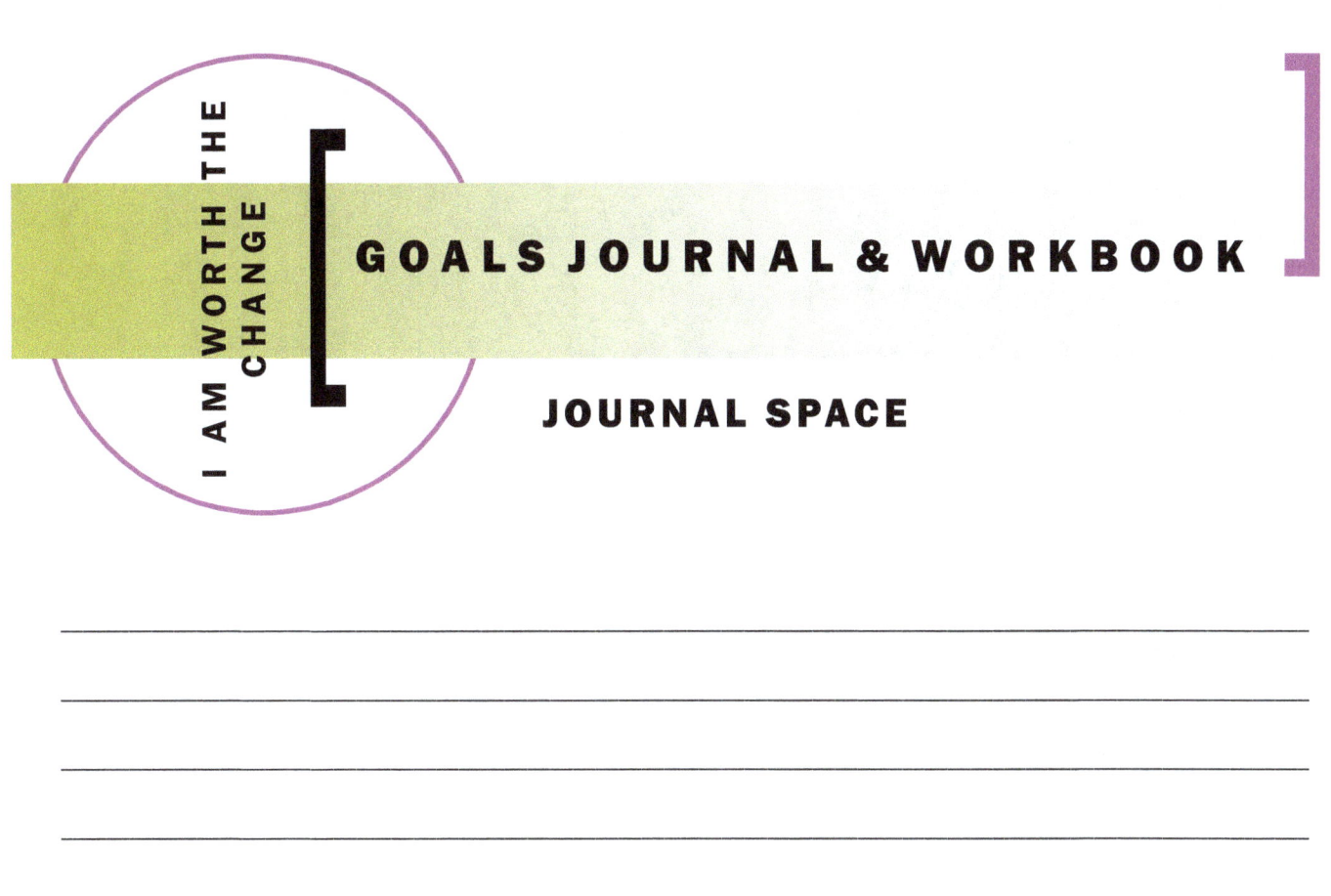

GOALS JOURNAL & WORKBOOK

JOURNAL SPACE

I AM WORTH THE CHANGE

Results:

GOAL:

SET DATE:

○ I MADE IT! LET'S CELEBRATE! ☐

○ I JUST NEED A LITTLE MORE TIME AND I GOT THIS! ☐

○ THIS IS NO LONGER A GOAL ☐

[CHECK IN]: HOW AM I FEELING?

_____
_____
_____
_____

LESSONS I LEARNED:

1. _____
2. _____
3. _____

WHAT DO I NEED TO GET TO THE FINISHED LINE?

☐ _____
☐ _____
☐ _____

I AM WORTH THE CHANGE

GOALS JOURNAL & WORKBOOK

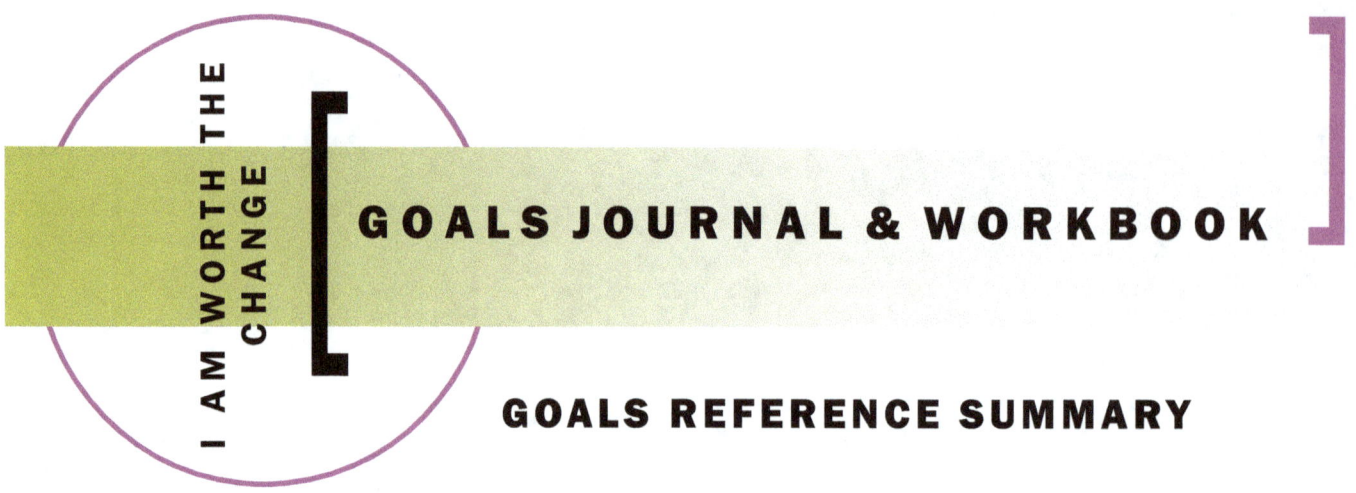

GOALS REFERENCE SUMMARY

	Goal	Challenge / Obstacle	Results after you overcome the challenge/obstacle
1			
2			
3			

GOALS JOURNAL & WORKBOOK

GOALS REFERENCE SUMMARY

	Goal	Challenge / Obstacle	Results after you overcome the challenge/obstacle
4			
5			
6			

GOALS REFERENCE SUMMARY

	Goal	Challenge / Obstacle	Results after you overcome the challenge/obstacle
7			
8			
9			

GOALS REFERENCE SUMMARY

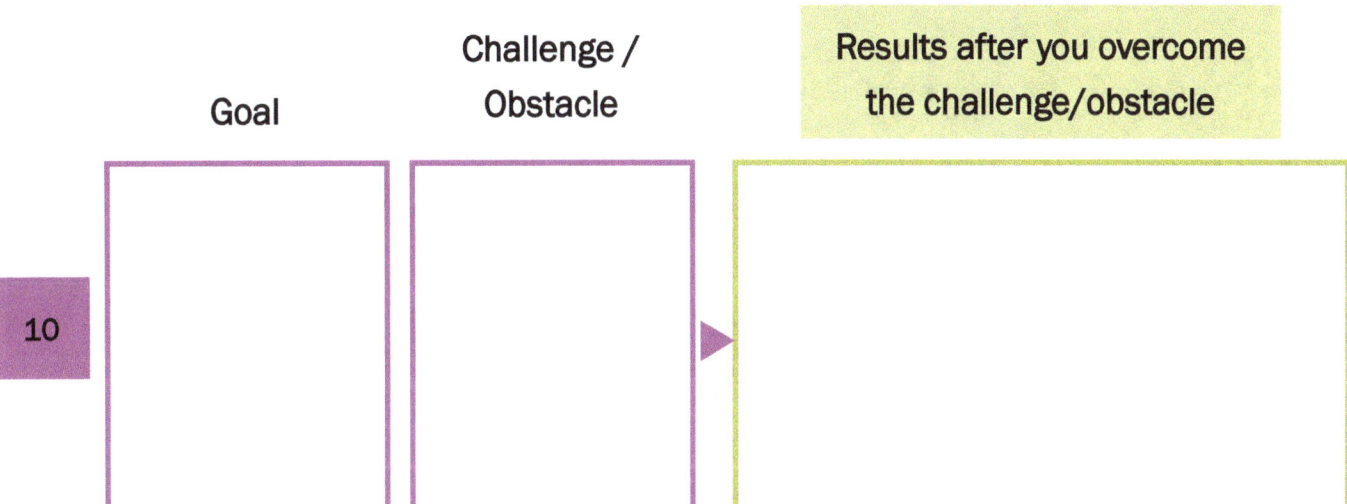

EMOTIONS GUIDE

☐ OPTIMISTIC	☐ CONFIDENT	☐ APPRECIATED	☐ RESTED
☐ PEACEFUL	☐ ENTHUSIASTIC	☐ ANOINTED	☐ SUCCESSFUL
☐ HAPPY / JOYFUL	☐ POWERFUL	☐ STRONG	☐ ENCOURAGED
☐ BOLD	☐ INSPIRED	☐ WISE	☐ ENERGIZED
☐ COURAGEOUS	☐ EXCITED	☐ CREATIVE	☐ SUPPORTED
☐ PATIENT	☐ CLEAR (CLARITY)	☐ PROSPEROUS	☐ HOPEFUL
☐ FULFILLED	☐ LOVED	☐ TRUSTING	☐ GRATEFUL
☐ ACCEPTED	☐ MOTIVATED	☐ SATISFIED	☐ SECURE / SAFE
☐ IT'S POSSIBLE!	☐ ADVENTUROUS	☐ THANKFUL	☐ CHEERFUL

GOALS JOURNAL & WORKBOOK

EMOTIONS GUIDE

☐ WORRIED	☐ LONELY	☐ EXHAUSTED	☐ SAD
☐ ANGRY	☐ DEPRESSED	☐ FRUSTRATED	☐ UNFULFILLED
☐ UNSUPPORTED	☐ NUMB	☐ DISCOURAGED	☐ STUCK
☐ CONFUSED	☐ LOST	☐ DRAINED	☐ IMPATIENT
☐ USED	☐ UNHEARD	☐ REGRETFUL	☐ ANNOYED
☐ BORED	☐ HURT	☐ UNDERVALUED	☐ UNAPPRECIATED
☐ UNSUCCESSFUL	☐ DISTRACTED	☐ SKEPTICAL	☐ PESSIMISTIC
☐ UNBELIEVING	☐ IGNORED	☐ BETRAYED	☐ DOUBTFUL
☐ RESENTMENT	☐ UNLOVED	☐ REJECTED	☐ GUARDED

EMOTIONS GUIDE

- [ ] UNRECOGNIZED
- [ ] SHAME
- [ ] INADEQUATE
- [ ] GUILT
- [ ] INTIMIDATED
- [ ] INFERIORITY
- [ ] EMBARRASSED
- [ ] UNCONFIDENT
- [ ] UNTRUSTING
- [ ] VULNERABLE
- [ ] LEERY
- [ ] UNWORTHY
- [ ] INSECURE
- [ ] ANXIOUS / ANXIETY
- [ ] AFRAID / FEAFFUL
- [ ] MISUNDERSTOOD
- [ ] I'M NOT SURE

COME SHARE YOUR GOALS, RESULTS & EXPERIENCE

One of the greatest parts of going through a process, meeting a goal, or experiencing an accomplishment, is having other people to share it with. You can celebrate your own success and I encourage you to do so, but if you want someone else to celebrate with you and congratulate you, pop over in my email and share your success with me! Let me know what happened! What goal did you set? What challenges did you overcome? What help did you get? Give me the deets!

I'm excited for you!

If you've enjoyed this goals journal and workbook, please let us know and if it has greatly encouraged and inspired you, please show us some love and leave a review on Amazon and share it with your friends and family.

If you don't want to stop here and would like to dig a little deeper, check out our course, also called, "I Am Worth the Change," that will take you further along in your journey!

www.kingdompurposeuniversity.com

connect@floydisepaquette.com

GOALS JOURNAL & WORKBOOK

ABOUT THE AUTHOR

Floydise Paquette is a prolific author with a variety of works published and yet to come. She is called and graced with a unique voice and powerful mandate to encourage, strengthen and build up God's people. Her gift of writing is being used to bring healing and restoration to the hearts of people around the world.

She is a mother, minister, writer, speaker, life coach and founder of Kingdom Purpose University.

Floydise has also written a book and small group engagement guide called, *Overcoming Jealousy in the Church & In Ministry*, which is sold on Amazon and various other online marketplaces.

Be on the look out for her soon to be released devotional journal called, *From Desperation to Destiny*.

CONNECT WITH FLOYDISE:

Website: www.floydisepaquette.com

Email: connect@floydisepaquette.com